A New True Book

SOIL EROSION AND POLLUTION

By Darlene R. Stille

CHILDRENS PRESS®

CHICAGO

Garbage dump

PHOTO CREDITS

AP/Wide World Photos — 11, 38

© Cameramann International Ltd. — 45

The Marilyn Gartman Agency — © Carl E. Krupp, 17 (right)

Historical Pictures Service, Chicago — 19 (left)

© Tom Messenger — 33 (bottom right)

© Norma Morrison — 6 (center)

© Chip and Rosa Maria de la Cueva Peterson — 6 (bottom right)

Photri — 13 (right), 15, 22, 23, 37 (left), 43 (2 photos)

R/C Photo Agency — © Earl L. Kubis, 16; © Richard L. Capps, 17 (left)

Root Resources — © Mary A. Root, Cover, 6 (left); © Kitty Kohout, 2, 4 (bottom left)

Shostal Associates/SuperStock International, Inc. — 19 (right); © Louis Van Camp, 6 (top right); © Gene Ahrens, 9; © Ernest Manewal, 12 (right); © Jerry Irwin, 13 (left); © Robin Smith, 18 (left); © Bill Barley, 35 (left); © Sal Maimone, 44 (right)

Tom Stack & Associates — © Gary Milburn, Cover, 35 (right); © Spencer Swanger, 4 (top left); © Bob Pool, 4 (top right); © David M. Dennis, 4 (bottom right); © Walt Anderson, 7 (left); © Jack Swenson, 7 (right), 25; © David M. Doody, 37 (right); © Tom Stack, 40 (left)

Third Coast Stock Source — © Steve Solum, 4 (top center)

Valan — © Wayne Lankinen, 4 (bottom center); © Phil Norton, 12 (left), 33 (left); © Thomas Kitchin, 17 (center), 18 (right); © Hälle Flygare Photos, Ltd., 21; © Jeff Foott, 27; © Kennon Cooke, 29 (left); © Karen D. Rooney, 29 (right); © Jean Bruneau, 33 (top right), 40 (right); © J. A. Wilkinson, 44 (left)

Art — 31 Courtesy of National Solid Wastes Management Association

Cover — Hazardous waste — © Gary Milburn
Rocky subsoil displaced by strip mining — © Mary A. Root

Library of Congress Cataloging-in-Publication Data

Stille, Darlene R.
  Soil erosion and pollution / by Darlene R. Stille.
    p.   cm. — (A New true book)
  Includes index.
  Summary: Discusses the erosion and pollution of soil, the harmful effects of these processes, and ways of preventing them.
  ISBN 0-516-01188-X
    1. Soil pollution — Juvenile literature. 2. Soil erosion — Juvenile literature. [1. Soil erosion. 2. Soil pollution. 3. Pollution.] I. Title.
TD878.S75   1990   89-25360
363.73'96 — dc20   CIP
                                               AC

TABLE OF CONTENTS

Most plants grow in
soil, and many animals
make their homes by
burrowing into soil.

WHAT IS SOIL?

All kinds of plants, from towering trees to tiny dandelions, grow in soil.

Many kinds of animals live in soil. Worms and insects live in the soil. Bacteria live there, too. And some larger animals, such as rabbits and prairie dogs, dig their burrows in the soil.

Houses and other buildings are built on the soil. In the country, farm crops are planted in the soil.

Vegetables and grains need soil. The cattle that give us meat depend on plants to live.

Vegetables and grains need soil. The cattle that give us meat depend on plants to live.

Most of our food comes from the soil. We eat fruits and vegetables that grow in the soil. We bake bread from wheat that grows in the soil. We drink the milk and eat the meat from animals that eat the plants growing in soil.

6

Severe erosion in Madagascar (left) exposes tree roots.
Hillsides (right) are especially susceptible to erosion.

Soil is very important. But soil can be damaged. Wind can blow soil away. Rain can wash soil away. This is called soil erosion.

Sometimes, dangerous chemicals get into the soil. This is called soil pollution. Pollution of the soil can be dangerous to our health.

WHERE SOIL COMES FROM

Sometimes we call soil "dirt." Sometimes we call it "earth." Sometimes we call it "the ground." Usually we never think about it at all because it is always there.

But soil has not always been there. When our planet first formed, there was no soil.

Soil gradually began to form as wind and water broke rocks into tiny pieces. Dead plants and animals

These rotting logs will decay and help make new soil.

decayed and became part of this early soil.

Soil is still being made today.

Soil forms in layers. The top layer is called the topsoil. Under the topsoil is the subsoil. And beneath these layers of soil is a layer of rock called the bedrock.

Some soils took millions of years to form. The deeper and richer the soil, the longer it took nature to make the soil.

Although soil took a very long time to develop, it can be destroyed in a very short time. If people are not careful, soil in some areas can be destroyed faster than nature can replace it.

HOW EROSION CAN HARM SOIL

Soil erosion caused severe problems in the southern Great Plains during the 1930s.

Soil erosion by wind and water has been a problem ever since people learned to farm about 8,000 years ago. Erosion is caused when people cut down trees and dig up grasses to plant crops. When people clear the land for crops, they

Flooding (above) causes erosion of farmland. Cutting down trees (right) destroys roots that hold the soil.

destroy the roots of trees and grasses that help keep the soil from being blown away by the wind or washed away by the rain.

Farmers have learned ways to slow the erosion of soil. They plant trees along the edges of fields to block the

A pattern called
contour plowing (left).
Planting trees in rows
called windbreaks (above)
helps slow wind erosion.

wind. They plow fields in
patterns that help stop the rain
from washing soil away.

But erosion is still a
serious problem. Billions
of tons of soil are lost every
year in the world because
of erosion.

HOW POLLUTION CAN HARM SOIL

Many chemicals also can pollute and harm soil.

Chemical fertilizers that farmers use can harm the soil. They contain large amounts of nutrients called phosphates and nitrogen. These help crops grow. But putting too much fertilizer on the soil can be harmful.

Sprays are used to kill weeds and insects that

Airplanes are used to spray large fields with chemicals.

might harm crops. But these sprays contain poisonous chemicals.

Too much of these sprays can also harm the soil. Some insect sprays, for example, kill the bacteria that live in the soil. These bacteria help keep the soil fertile.

15

The praying mantis eats many insects that harm crops.

For these reasons, scientists are looking for better ways to control weeds and insects. One way is to use insects that do not harm crop plants. These insects eat other insects and weeds that can destroy crops.

One of the worst threats to soil in some areas today is pollution caused by harmful industrial chemicals.

Toxic chemicals can seep into the soil from open-air dumps.

Harmful chemicals can get into soil in a number of ways. They may be dumped onto the land as wastes from factories. They may come from garbage dumps. Once these chemicals get into soil, they are very difficult to get out.

17

Fumes from industrial plants can kill vegetation (left).
Polluted water from streams (right) can seep into the soil.

Plants take up these
harmful chemicals through
their roots. In soil that has
been heavily polluted with
poisonous chemicals, no
plants will grow.

GARBAGE DUMPS AND SOIL POLLUTION

The earliest type of soil
pollution came from
garbage dumps. As long as
people can remember,
garbage has been thrown
into open dumps. Then

Garbage dumps in 19th-century England (left) and in the U.S.A. today (right)

people learned that these open, smelly garbage pits spread germs. Rats and flies breed in garbage dumps.

So garbage was either burned or carried off to a new type of garbage dump called a landfill. In a landfill, a layer of soil is spread over each new layer of garbage. Under the soil, the garbage decays. This method prevents smells and keeps down the number of rats and flies, but it creates another problem.

A bulldozer pushes a layer of soil over the garbage in a landfill.

Landfills that are not tightly sealed lead to soil pollution. This is because garbage contains many things that are dangerous. Household batteries, for example, contain metals, such as

Garbage dumps sealed with dirt layers are called sanitary landfills.

mercury or lead, that are very poisonous.

Rainwater or water trapped in the garbage seeps through the landfill. The water picks up metals and harmful chemicals and carries them down through

Water soaks down through the layers of a landfill.

the landfill and into the
surrounding soil.

The pollutants can then
travel down through the
various layers of soil and
into the water that lies
underground. Once this
water has been polluted,
there is no way to clean it up.

TOXIC-WASTE DUMPS

Another source of soil pollution is the hazardous-waste, or toxic-waste, dump. Many kinds of dangerous chemicals are stored in toxic-waste dumps. The harmful chemicals come from paper mills, metal-plating companies, paint factories, plastics manufacturers, oil refineries, chemical plants, insect- and weed-spray companies, and other factories.

These drums may rust away and leak their toxic contents into the soil.

Some of these chemicals
can explode, causing
serious fires, and releasing
deadly fumes into the air.
Toxic-waste dumps are
usually found on vacant
land. The dangerous wastes

are often placed in metal storage containers. Sometimes these containers are buried underground.

Over time, the containers begin to rust. The dangerous chemicals leak out into the ground.

If the chemicals are highly poisonous, they pollute the soil and they eventually pollute the underground water supply.

Stricter laws against pollution must be made and enforced.

HOW SOIL POLLUTION CAN HARM US

Dangerous chemicals that get into the soil can sometimes get into our bodies and cause birth defects or diseases such as cancer.

Poisonous chemicals in the soil may send vapors, or gases, into the air. People may breathe in these harmful vapors.

Some harmful chemicals can go through the skin. If people touch soil that is polluted with dangerous chemicals, their skin may absorb the poison.

If plants take up harmful chemicals from the soil, these chemicals could be passed on to people who eat the plants.

But there is a greater health risk when people eat animals that have eaten such plants. Harmful chemicals tend to build up in animals. People eating meat or drinking milk from animals that have eaten these plants will also take in the chemicals.

Harmful chemicals become concentrated in animals that eat polluted plants.

NEW WAYS OF HANDLING GARBAGE

We can prevent soil pollution from garbage.

We can bury garbage safely in landfills that are lined with concrete or hard-packed clay. Safe landfills have pipes and pumps to remove any water that might seep through the garbage and collect pollutants. This water, called leachate, is then brought to wastewater-treatment plants.

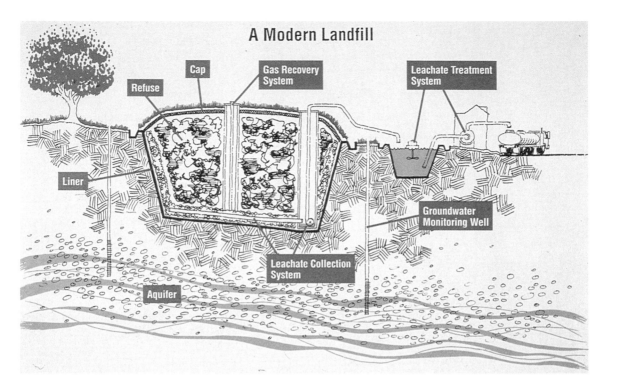

A Modern Landfill

Refuse
Cap
Gas Recovery System
Leachate Treatment System
Liner
Groundwater Monitoring Well
Leachate Collection System
Aquifer

Garbage can be burned,
but special incinerators
must be built to prevent
harmful chemicals from
escaping in smoke or gas.

The poisonous ash from
the garbage must be
collected and buried in

specially lined pits. The ash can also be sealed in cement or glass and buried.

Recycling is one of the best ways to help prevent soil pollution by garbage.

Paper can be recycled easily, as can glass bottles and metal cans. Scientists are trying to find ways of recycling other things, such as plastic.

Trash and garbage that has been recycled does not need to

In areas that do recycling, people must use separate containers for glass, paper, plastic, and cans.

be buried or burned. Recycled garbage can be used again and again. It does not go into landfills and pollute the soil.

CLEANING UP THE DUMPS

It is very expensive to clean up polluted soil.

Usually, all the polluted soil must be dug up. Then it is taken to a place where the dangerous chemicals can be removed safely. Sometimes the soil is heated to make the chemicals evaporate. Sometimes the soil is mixed with other chemicals that make the poisonous chemicals harmless.

Scientists are trying to find

An industrial waste treatment plant (left).
Contaminated soil (right) must be disposed of carefully.

less expensive ways of
cleaning up toxic wastes.
Someday the polluted soil
might be treated where it is.
Pipes could be put down
into the ground to heat the
soil. The vapors given off
could be collected by a
system of ducts and fans.

RADIATION FROM THE SOIL

A special type of
dangerous material, called
radioactive material, can get
into the soil. Radioactive
material sends out invisible
but very dangerous rays.
These rays can go through
the floors and walls of
ordinary buildings. They can
also damage the cells in
people's bodies.

This type of pollution is
usually caused by activities
involving atomic weapons or
nuclear power plants. It has

Technicians (right) monitor radioactivity that may be
released by a nuclear power plant's cooling towers.

also been caused by the
dumping of radioactive
wastes from uranium mines.

Most radioactive pollution
of the soil is accidental.
Such pollution can come
from leaks at plants that
process radioactive material.

The nuclear power plant at Chernobyl, Soviet Union, after the 1986 explosion

Very serious soil pollution in Europe and the Soviet Union was caused by an explosion at a Soviet plant in 1986. The explosion released radioactive dust and smoke, and wherever this radioactive material fell to earth, it polluted the soil.

But not all radioactive soil is caused by nuclear accidents. One radioactive substance—radon—comes from nature.

Radon is a radioactive gas. It gives off harmful rays that can damage body cells. Radon can cause lung cancer and other diseases.

Radon occurs naturally in some types of soil and rock. It can be found in bricks made from clay that contains radon.

Very little indoor air can escape from a tightly sealed building.
Air ducts (right) and fans keep fresh air circulating through a house.

In the past, radon was usually not dangerous to people. But radon has become a problem because many houses and other buildings today are tightly sealed to save energy.

But a tightly sealed house can trap radon inside.

The simplest way to get rid of radon that is already inside a house is to open the windows.

But opening windows during cold weather wastes energy. So homes built on soil that contains too much radon need special treatment.

Special air ducts, fans, and vents can be installed that keep fresh air circulating through the house and keep the harmful radon from building up.

PROTECTING OUR SOIL

The best way to deal with soil pollution is to prevent it from happening in the first place.

In most countries, open garbage dumps are no longer allowed. Also, landfills that let chemicals seep into the ground are being closed down.

Cities and towns are finding new ways to deal with garbage. Some garbage now goes into sealed

Garbage incinerator (left) in Virginia. Radioactive wastes (above) are sometimes buried in concrete boxes.

landfills, some is burned in special incinerators, and some is recycled.

There are laws that say how harmful chemical wastes from factories must be handled. They can no longer be dumped on vacant land and left to pollute the soil and the water supply.

Modern high-yield agriculture is dependent on chemical pesticides, but these substances may harm the soil.

There are laws about chemicals that are sprayed on crops to kill weeds and insects. These chemicals must be tested to be sure they do not cause diseases. Also, these chemicals must disappear from the soil quickly. Long-lasting chemicals can pollute the soil.

Trees and grasses protect the soil from erosion.

Soil must also be protected. Trees and grasses must be planted to prevent erosion.

It took nature a very long time to make the soil, so we must make sure that the soil stays around for a very long time in the future.

45

WORDS YOU SHOULD KNOW

ash(ASH) — the grayish, powdery matter that remains after something has been burned

bacteria(back • TEER • ee • ya) — tiny living things that have only one cell and can be seen only with a microscope

bedrock(BEHD • rahk) — the solid rock layer under the soil

birth defect(BERTH DEE • fekt) — a disease or handicap that a baby has at birth

chemicals(KEM • ih • kuls) — materials that are used in fertilizers and in many manufacturing processes and that are often harmful to living things

decay(dih • KAY) — the process of rotting or breaking down by the action of bacteria

erosion(ih • ROH • zhun) — the wearing away of the land, caused by the action of wind and water

fertilizers(FER • tih • lye • zerz) — materials that contain nutrients to help plants grow

germs(JERMZ) — harmful bacteria that cause diseases

incinerator(in • SIN • er • ray • ter) — a place where solid waste material such as garbage is burned

landfill(LAND • fil) — a dump where waste matter is deposited in layers and the layers are covered with soil to seal the garbage from the air

leachate(LEE • chayt) — liquid wastes that come from garbage in a landfill

nitrogen(NYE • troh • jin) — a gas in the air; a nutrient that is needed by plants to grow

nuclear power(NOO • clee • er POW • er) — electric power that is generated in nuclear plants that use the heat from radioactive elements as a source of energy

nutrient(NOO • tree • ent) — food

phosphates(FAHSS • faytes) — nutrients that are needed by plants to grow

pollution(puh • LOO • shun) — the dirtying of the earth's air, water, and land

radioactive(ray • dee • oh • AK • tihv) — giving off energy in the form of rays or particles

radon(RAY • dahn) — a radioactive gas found in the soil

recycling(ree • SYE • kling) — saving things and using them over and over again

subsoil(SUHB • soyl) — the layer of soil that is found below the topsoil and that has few plant nutrients and little organic matter

topsoil(TAHP • soyl) — the layer of soil that is found at the top of the ground and that is rich in plant nutrients and organic matter

toxic waste(TAHX • ik WAYST) — poisonous waste from factories and other businesses

INDEX

About the Author

Darlene R. Stille is a Chicago-based science writer and editor.

J